BOOK OF FIQH
& MANNERS
FOR KIDS
BOOK 1

© Saudi Arabia Curriculum , 2020

Tawheed for Kids Class 1. /
- Al Madinah Al Munawwarah , 2020
63p ; ..cm
ISBN: 978-179-18-6180-3
1- Tauhid 2- Islamic theology I-Title
240 dc 1441/6987
L.D. no. 1441/6987
ISBN: 978-179-18-6180-3

This book is based on the Saudi Arabian Curriculum which is taught in all the primary schools in the KSA. It covers the full series of authentic Islamic knowledge through the primary school ages. It is important for all kids to have knowledge of these matters.

The full series consists of books on Tawheed, Fiqh and Hadeeth for all primary school years.

Email: alfurqanebooks@gmail.com

BOOK OF FIQH
& MANNERS
FOR KIDS
BOOK 1

SAUDI ARABIA CURRICULUM

Contents

بسم الله الرحمن الرحيم

Bismillah – means to start in the name of Allah seeking the help from Allah and the blessings from Allah.

Ar-Rahman- means Allah has mercy on all of his creation, Allah provides food and water for all of His creation. Allah has given many blessings to all of his slaves. So we should always thank Allah for these blessings, we can hear, talk, walk, see, eat, think and many endless blessings.

Ar-Raheem- this is the special mercy that Allah has for his slaves who worship him upon Tawheed. They worship Allah alone without making any partners with Allah.

Love for the Quran

Quran is the **speech of Allah**.

A small boy called Umar went to the Masjid with his father; he saw the Quran on the floor, so he picked it up and placed it on the shelves. Then Umar sat quietly next to his father listening to the Quran. When listening to the Quran, you have to stop talking.

How do we respect the Quran?

Before touching the Quran then we should make Wudu (ablution).

When we are about to read the Quran, then we say

I seek refuge in Allah from the accursed Shaytaan (Devil).

And at the start of the first surah, then we say

بسم الله الرحمن الرحيم

We stay silent and listen to the recitation of the Quran.

We do not play or speak during the recitation of the Quran.

We put the Quran in a place which is suitable for it.

Colour with the green pencil the correct manner.

Colour with the red pencil the wrong manner.

Writing and drawing in the Mushaf (Quran)
To memorize the Quran
To recite the Quran in a nice melodious voice
To put the Mushaf (Quran) on the floor

Complete the following sentence:

I love the ....

I read the Noble Quran ....

If you saw your brother with some pages from the Noble Quran in his drawer, then how should you help him? Choose one from the 3 choices below, colour it with a red pencil.

Colour this sentence:

Alhamdulillah I learnt how to respect the Noble Quran

From the Life of Our Prophet Muhammad ﷺ may the peace and blessings of Allah be upon him.

• He is truthful

- He is trustworthy

- He is brave

1. Give the pages to the teacher

2. Leave the pages in the drawer

3. Remind him of what we learnt on how to respect the Quran

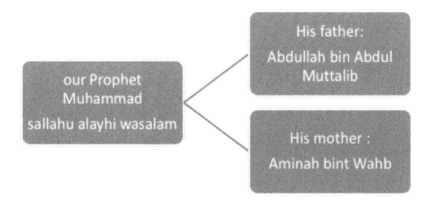

He was born in the city of Makkah Al-Mukarramah (the Honored Makkah); he was 40 years old when he got the Prophethood. Allah the Most Merciful sent him to all of the mankind to call them to the religion of Islaam- to worship Allah alone and not to make any Shirk with Allah. He migrated from Makkah to Madinah and died in Madinah at the age of 63.

I love our Prophet Muhammad ﷺ and I obey him. The people described our Prophet ﷺ with good character, for indeed he was

- Truthful

- Brave

- Trustworthy

He always had mercy on the poor and the weak people and used to feel sorry for them.

How he was trustworthy?

The Messenger of Allah Muhammad ﷺ was known among the people as "Ameen" (the trustworthy one). His people used to call him "Ameen" and the people used to leave their expensive things and their money with the Messenger of Allah ﷺ. So when he decided to make Hijrah (migration to Madinah from Makkah) he asked his cousin, Ali bin Abee Talib (may Allah be pleased with him) to return all the items back to their owners.

How was he truthful?

When Allah the Most High commanded the Prophet ﷺ to call his relatives to worship Allah alone, he climbed the mount Safa in Makkah Al-Mukarramah. He called his relatives, so they all gathered around him. Abu Lahab also came, who is the uncle of the Prophet ﷺ. So the Messenger of Allah ﷺ asked all of them "if I informed you that a group of people in the valley wants to attack you, would you believe me?'. So they all replied "Yes, indeed we have never heard from you a lie". Then he said "Indeed I came to warn all of you that in front of you is a terrible punishment (by Allah).

How was the Prophet ﷺ brave?

When the Muslims met the Mushrikeen (people of Shirk disbelievers) in the battle of Badr, the Mushrikeen were greater in number than the Muslims and they had more weapons also. So the Messenger of Allah ﷺ was the bravest person in this battle, he was at the front line directly facing the enemy. He was the strongest person on the battlefield.

All Praise is due to Allah (Alhamdulillaah) we learnt:

- We follow the way of the Prophet ﷺ in his actions and his speech.

- To return the trust (things, property, money, gold, silver, cars, etc) of others to them.

- To be truthful in my speech

- To be brave in speaking the truth.

- When the Prophet ﷺ name is mentioned then we send sallam and salutations on him by saying

صلى الله عليه وسلم

Connect from Table A to what is correct from Table B

I love the Prophet ﷺ	To hit your small brother
I hate	Then return it back
It is **not** brave	So I obey him
If you see a poor person	**Lying**
If you borrow something	Then quickly help him and be kind to him

As-salaam

Means: may the Peace, mercy of Allah and the blessings of Allah be upon you. It is a Dua (prayer) asking Allah to protect, have mercy and bless your Muslim brother.

The teacher said to his students:

Shall I show you a way where you can earn a lot of reward (from Allah) and the people will love you?

So the students replied:

Yes, Oh our teacher.

The teacher said:

It is the greeting of As-salam, when you meet someone you say to them

"Asalaamu Alaikum Wa Rehmatullahi Wabarakatahu"

So Ahmed said:

Shall I give Salam to those who I do not know.

The teacher replied:

Yes, we give Salam to those we know and those we do not know.

Khalid said: How do we reply back to the Salaam.

The teacher replied, we say:

"wa Alaikum salaam wa Rehmatullah Wabarakatahu ".

Virtue of Salaam

A man came to the Prophet (ﷺ) and said: "As-Salamu 'Alaikum (May you be safe from evil). Messenger of Allah (ﷺ) responded to his greeting and the man sat down. The Prophet (ﷺ) said, "Ten (meaning the man had earned the merit of ten good acts)." Another one came and said: "As-Salamu 'Alaikum wa Rehmatullah (may you be safe from evil, and Mercy of Allah be upon you)." Messenger of Allah (ﷺ) responded to his greeting and the man sat down. Messenger of Allah (ﷺ) said, "Twenty." A third one came and said: "As-Salamu 'Alaikum wa Rahmatullahi wa Barakatuhu (may you be safe from evil, and the Mercy of Allah and His Blessings be upon you)." Messenger of Allah (ﷺ) responded to his greeting and the man sat down. Messenger of Allah (ﷺ) said, "Thirty." [Abu Dawud and At- Tirmidhi]

Connect the two together to give right answer.

Asalaamu Alaikum wa Rahmatullahi wa Barakatuhu

Asalamu Alaikum

Asalaamu Alaikum wa Rahmatullahi

Which answer makes me happy?

When my brother enters the home and he says: ☐

How are you, my dear mother? ☐

Asalaamu Alaikum **wa Rahmatullahi wa Barakatuhu, how are you, my dear mother?**

Which action will please you?

When the student enters the classroom and....

He walks to his seat and sits on it. ☐

He says As-salaam Alaikum wa Rahmatullahi wa Barakatuhu, then walks to his seat and sits on it. ☐

My brother phoned his friend

and I was happy when he said

Where is Abdullah?   ☐

Asalaamu Alaikum wa Rahmatullahi wa Barakatuhu, where is Abdullah?   ☐

Kindness to parents
Do you kiss the head of your father?

Kindness to parents is the way to Paradise.

Allah ordered us in the Quran:

وَقَضَى رَبُّكَ أَلَّا تَعْبُدُوا إِلَّا إِيَّاهُ وَبِالْوَالِدَيْنِ إِحْسَانًا

And your Lord has decreed (commanded, ordered) that you not worship except Him, and to be kind with your parents.[Surah Al-Israa:23]

The Messenger of Allah

ordered us to be kind with our parents.

A person came to Messenger of Allah (ﷺ) and asked, "Who among people is most deserving of my fine treatment?" He (ﷺ) said, "Your mother". He again asked, "Who next?" "Your mother", the Prophet (ﷺ) replied again. He asked, "Who next?" He (the Prophet (ﷺ)) said again, "Your mother." He again asked, "Then who?" Thereupon he (ﷺ) said," Then your father."(Bukhari and Muslim)

The students said:

"We want to go on this path so that we reach Paradise".

So the teacher said:

Being kind to your parents is done through many ways such as:

To obey your parents. When they ask you for something then reply kindly "Yes certainly my Mother/Father".

Ask their permission before you enter into their room.

Give them salaam by saying to them:

Asalaamu Alaikum wa Rahmatullahi wa Barakatuhu.

Let them enter or leave first.

Lower your voice while talking to them and do not shout at them.

Make them happy by doing that which pleases them so happiness enters their heart.

All praise is due to Allah, I have learnt how to please my parents.

Tick the boxes with ☑ or ☒

I was happy when the student said

Father, I had a very good day at the school today ☐

Asalaamu Alaikum wa Rahmatullahi wa Barakatuhu, Father, I had a very good

day at the school today ☐

What do we do, when we enter upon our parents?

Do we knock on the door? ☐

Do we enter the room without asking permission? ☐

Colour the following sentence:

I love my mother and my father

I obey my mother and my father

How to respect the teacher?

Who teaches you in the classroom?

- I learn the rights of my teacher:

- I give Salaam to him.

- I do not speak when he is speaking

- I listen to him when he is talking

- I speak to him with good manners

- I pray for him

Our teacher taught us:

- Ask for permission before entering or leaving the classroom.

- Complete the homework from the school.

- Look after my books and my things.

- Have good manners when asking or

replying or working or playing.

I am happy when the student says to the teacher:

Excuse me, teacher, am I allowed going out and drinking water. ☐

I am going out of the classroom to drink water. ☐

Manners: using a bathroom.

Islaam is a religion which teaches us how to be clean and purify ourselves.

We learnt how to go to the bathroom;

do you remember anything regarding it?

I say when I enter the bathroom

بسم اللَّه ـ اللهم إني أعوذ بك من الخبث والخبائث

The meaning is: Oh Allah, I seek refuge in you from the male and female devils.

I do not speaking to anyone while I am in the bathroom.

After using the toilet. I clean myself using the left hand with water or stones or tissues.

While leaving the bathroom, I say

غفرانك

Grant me your forgiveness (oh Allah)

Colour this sentence:

I am a Muslim and I keep my body and my clothes clean and pure and I keep the bathroom clean after using it.

Semester 2

بسم الله الرحمن الرحيم

Name these things

Cleanliness and purification

Firstly purification

والدليل قول الله تعالي: وثيابك فطهر

And your garments purify!

Cleanliness   purification

This is called Istinjaa

اِسْتِنْجَاءً

I clean my private parts till all the impurities are removed

I clean the two passages (from the front and back) with tissues or stones until the impurities are removed

This is called Istijmaar

استِجْمَارًا

We learnt that when we go to the bathroom then we say:

Firstly purification Purification Cleanliness

(بِسْمِ اللهِ اللّٰهُمَّ إِنِّي
أَعُوذُ بِكَ مِنَ الْخُبُثِ
وَالْخَبَائِثِ)‏

When entering he says: In the name of Allah Oh Allah I seek refuge with you from the filthy male and female Jinn

(غُفْرَانَكَ)‏

While leaving then say: I seek forgiveness (from Allah)

Purification

Removing the impurities	Wudu (ablution)

With water

- Body

- Clothes

- And place of prayer

It is obligated to make Wudu with pure clean water before prayer

Prayer area

body

Cleanliness

Always stay clean since our religion Islaam requires us to Water is a blessing from Allah

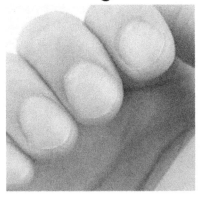

I always cut my nails

I clean my thobe whenever it becomes dirty

Water is a blessing from Allah

How can we save water?

_____

_____

_____

_____

_____

_____

_____

_____

Islaam is built on 5 pillars

The proof of the 5 pillars is the saying of the Prophet ﷺ:

'Islam is built upon five [pillars]: testifying that there is none worthy of worship except Allah and that Muhammad is the Messenger of Allah, establishing the prayers, giving zakat, making pilgrimage to the House and fasting the month of Ramadan.'" (Bukhari and Muslim).

What are the 5 Pillars?

1. -------------------------------------

2. -------------------------------------

3. -------------------------------------

4. -------------------------------------

5. -------------------------------------

Wudu is worship of Allah

The Messenger of Allah ﷺ said "Whoever performs the Wudu perfectly then his sins will depart from his body even from under his nails.

I say: Bismillah (in the name of Allah)

I wash my hands three times

I rinse the mouth and clean the nose three times

I wash my face three times

I wash my both hands up to the elbow

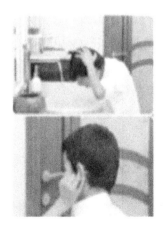

Wipe the heads and cleans the ears once

I wash my feet up to the ankles three times

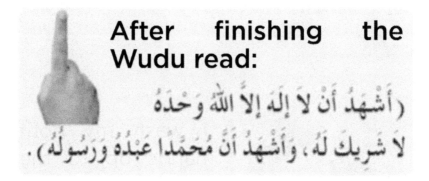

After finishing the Wudu read:

(أَشْهَدُ أَنْ لاَ إِلَهَ إِلاَّ اللهُ وَحْدَهُ

لاَ شَرِيكَ لَهُ، وَأَشْهَدُ أَنَّ مُحَمَّدًا عَبْدُهُ وَرَسُولُهُ) .

I bear witness that none has the right to be worshipped except Allah alone He has no partners and I bear witness that Muhammed is his slave and his Messenger

I do not waste water

Write the numbers in the correct sequence of Wudu

I wash my feet up to the ankles

I wash my face

I wash my hands

I wipe my head and ears

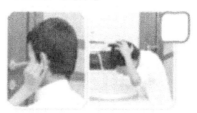

I rinse my mouth and clean my nose

I wash my hands to the elbow

Circle the area that needs to be washed and write under the picture

 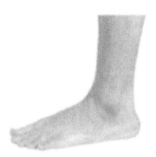

Colour the following Dua which is said after completing the Wudu.

أَشْهَدُ أَنْ لَا إِلٰهَ إِلَّا اللّٰهُ
وَحْدَهُ لَا شَرِيكَ لَهُ وَأَشْهَدُ
أَنَّ مُحَمَّدًا عَبْدُهُ وَرَسُولُهُ

The obligatory Prayers

How many times do you hear the Adhan every day?

The Prayer is the second pillar of Islam after the 'testimony of the faith'

There are 5 obligatory prayers every day

1- Fajr

2 Rakah

2-Dhuhr

4 Rakah

3- Asr

2 Rakah

4-Magrib

3 Rakah

5-Ishaa

4 Rakah

I pray in order to obey Allah and His Messenger ﷺ

The Messenger of Allaah (peace and blessings of Allaah be upon him) said: "One prayer in my mosque is better than one thousand prayers elsewhere, except al-Masjid al-Haraam, and one prayer in al-Masjid al-Haraam is better than one hundred thousand prayers elsewhere." Narrated by Ahmad and Ibn Majah.

Manner of Praying

The Muslims offer the Prayers in the same manner

Why?

How should I pray?

The Messenger of Allah ﷺ said "Pray as you have seen me pray"

I follow the Messenger ﷺ in my method of praying.

 Face the Qiblah

Say the opening Takbeer "Allahu Akbar"

I place my right hand over the left hand on the chest

I read the opening Dua

Then I read Surah Al-Fatiha and whatever I have memorized from the Quran

Meaning of the opening Dua

Glory is to You O Allah, and praise. Blessed is Your Name and Exalted is Your Majesty. There is none worthy of worship but You.

I will practice what I have learnt

Manner of Praying

I want to pray?

Which direction should I face?

What should I say at the opening Takbeer?

What shall i say after the opening Takbeer?

After reading Surah Al-Fatiha and some Ayaat from the Quran

I say Allah Akbar and make Ruku and read this 3 times in Arabic:

Glory be to my great Lord

سُبْحَانَ رَبِّيَ العَظِيمِ

I return from Ruku and say:

Allah listens to him who praises Him. Praise be to You, Our Rabb

سَمِعَ اللَّه لِمَنْ حَمِدَهُ رَبَّنَا وَلَكَ الحَمْدُ

Allah listens to him who praises Him. Praise be to You, Our Rabb

I say Allah Akbar and then make Sujood and read three times

Glory is to my Lord, the Most High.

Then I say Allah Akbar and sit up and read the following Dua between the 2 Sujood

رَبِّ اغْفِرْلِي رَبِّ اغْفِرْلِي

My Lord forgive me, my Lord forgive me

Then I say Allah Akbar and make Sujood the second time

3 Times سُبْحَانَ رَبِيَ الأَعْلَى

I practice what I learnt from the manner of Praying

What do I say while in state of Ruku?

What do I say while standing up from Ruku?

When I sit between the 2 Sujood what do I say?

After the second Sujood, I stand up by saying Allahu Akbar

Then I repeat exactly what I did in the first Rakah

التحيّاتُ لله والصلواتُ والطيباتُ السَّلامُ عليك أَيُّهَا النَّبيُّ وَرَحْمَةُ الله وَبَرَكاتُهُ السَّلامُ عَلَيْنَا وَعلى عبَاد الله الصَّالحين.

أَشْهَدُ أَنَّ لَا إِلَه إِلاَّ الله وَأَشْهَدُ أَنَّ مُحَمَّدًا عَبْدُهُ وَرَسُولُهُ

After the second Rakah I sit and read this Tashahud

All compliments, prayers and pure words are due to Allah. Peace be upon you, O Prophet, and the mercy of Allah and His blessings. Peace be upon us and upon the righteous slaves of Allah. I bear witness that there is no deity worthy of worship except Allah and I bear witness that Muhammad is His slave and Messenger

After reading the first Tashahud then I stand up for the third Rakah

I do what I did in the previous 2 Rakah however this time I only read Surah Al-Fatiha

I sit at the end of the 4th Rakah and read the Tashahud and send Salaam upon the Prophet ﷺ

التَّحِيَّاتُ لله والصلواتُ والطيباتُ السَّلامُ عليك أيُّهَا النَّبِيُّ وَرَحْمَةُ اللهِ وَبَرَكَاتُهُ السَّلامُ عَلَيْنَا وَعَلَى عِبَادِ اللهِ الصَّالحِين.

أَشْهَدُ أَنَّ لا إله إلاَّ الله وَأَشْهَدُ أَنَّ مُحَمَّدًا عَبْدُهُ وَرَسُولُهُ

اللَّهُمَّ صَلِّ عَلَى مُحَمَّد وَعَلَى آل مُحَمَّد ۞ كَمَا صَلَّيْتَ عَلَى ابْرَاهِيْمَ وَعَلَى آل ابْرَاهِيْمَ ۞ إنَّكَ حَمِيْدٌ مَجِيْدٌ ۞ اللَّهُمَّ بَارِكْ عَلَى مُحَمَّد وَعَلَى آل مُحَمَّد ۞ كَمَا بَارَكْتَ عَلَى ابْرَاهِيْمَ وَعَلَى آل ابْرَاهِيْمَ ۞ إنَّكَ حَمِيْدٌ مَجِيْدٌ

I give Salaam to the right and then the left by saying:

O Allah, send prayers upon Muhammad and upon the family of Muhammad, as You sent prayers upon Ibraaheem and the family of Ibraaheem, You are indeed Worthy of Praise, Full of Glory. O Allah, bless Muhammad and the family of Muhammad as You blessed Ibraaheem and the family of Ibraaheem, You are indeed Worthy of Praise, Full of Glory

Things which break the Prayer

Connect A to the correct answer from B

A

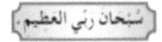
سُبْحَانَ رَبِّيَ الْعَظِيمِ.

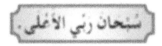
سُبْحَانَ رَبِّيَ الْأَعْلَى.

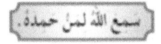
سَمِعَ اللهُ لِمَنْ حَمِدَهُ.

اللهُ أَكْبَرُ.

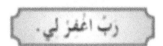
رَبِّ اغْفِرْ لِي.

B

Sujood

Ruku

Between the 2 Sujood

Standing up from Ruku

Al-Fatiha
(The opening Surah)

Al-Fatiha: umm-ul-Quran (mother of the Quran)

Why is Surah al-Fatiha so special?

Al-Fatiha is the opening chapter of the Quran; it is also named as the "Mother of the Quran". Al-Fatiha has the general meanings of all the glorious Quran. It is used as a Ruqya to treat pain from

Snake bite or a scorpion. It will remove the pain and the poison if the person has strong belief and depends upon Allah from his heart.

To know how important Surah Al-Fatiha is, then know that Allah will not accept your 5 daily prayers, if you did not recite this great Surah. This is the greatest Surah of the Quran.

Surah Al-Fatiha has many different names, some of them are:

Umm-al-Quran -which means "mother of the Quran"?

Al-Fatiha – the opening of the Quran

We will look at one story from the Hadith (sayings of the Messenger of Allah ﷺ) to show how important this surah really is. We should always remember the meanings when we recite this Surah.

Let's learn the meanings of Surah Al-Fatiha

بِسْمِ اللهِ الرَّحْمَنِ الرَّحِيمِ

(1) In the name of Allah, the Entirely Merciful, the Especially Merciful.

Means – We start with every beautiful name of Allah.

Allah has many names such as Al-Rahman meaning the one who is merciful to all of mankind.

Also the name Al-Raheem means one who is merciful to all the believers of Allah, who submit their will to Allah and are called Muslims. The Muslims do what Allah wants them to do, performing good actions so they get close to Allah.

When you say Bismillah, then you ask Allah to bless you and ask Allah to help you. So always when you start to eat, drink or write or anything else, then

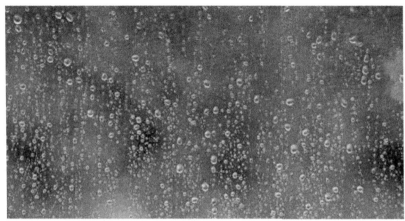

start with this word, Bismillah.

The rain is a mercy from Allah, it keep's everything alive. Water is needed to stay alive, humans need water and plants need water. Allah is in complete control of the rain and it will only rain when Allah has decreed it to rain.

الْحَمْدُ لِلَّهِ رَبِّ الْعَالَمِينَ

(2) [All] praise is [due] to Allah, Lord of the worlds –

Means: That we Muslims thank Allah for everything He has given us, and He has also given everything to all that exists from Mankind, Jinn and the Animals.

Allah has given us food, drink, health, eyesight, intelligence and every blessing in this world.

Allah created everything like the Mankind, the Sun, the Moon, the stars, the rain, the mountains, the rivers and everything else which exists. And he owns everything which exists and He is in control of everything that exists. So Allah sends down the rain from the sky, the rain makes the earth fertile so crops can grow. The Sun bakes the crops so they grow fast and are ready. The people eat from the fruits of the tree, the milk from the cows and everything else. Allah alone controls all of this, if there was no rain from the Sky the plants will die. If there was no Sunlight of the Sun the crops will not grow. So indeed it is Allah alone who is our Provider.

When Allah sends the rain from the Sky and the Sun which Allah created gives

sunlight to the tree. It makes the tree grow big and then fruit is grown on the tree. So there are oranges, apples, dates and many other fruits. Allah provides for all of us.

الرَّحْمَنِ الرَّحِيمِ

(3) The Entirely Merciful, the Especially Merciful,

Allah gives food, drink, security to the entire world, everything which is alive. This is from his Mercy.

On the day of Judgement he will show His Mercy to His believing Slaves, those who believed in Allah, those who did good deeds, those who prayed, those who fasted, those who gave charity, and those who went to the House of Allah, Makkah.

The Muslims travel to Makkah to perform Umrah and Hajj. The religion of Islaam is a mercy; it teaches us everything from being good to our parents, our neighbor's, and our friends. It teaches us how to worship Allah. Allah created us for one reason only- to worship Allah.

(4) Owner of the Day of Recompense.

The real owner of everything that exists

is Allah alone, everything other than Allah will die and they own their stuff for the time they are alive only. But Allah created everything, provided for all of them and Allah is the owner. Allah is also the one who will decide on the day of Judgement, when everyone will be rewarded or punished. Whoever believed in Allah and did not make anyone equal to Allah, or a partner with Allah and did good deeds will enter the gardens of paradise. Whoever did not believe in Allah and did evil deeds will enter the Hellfire. The Judgement is for Allah alone.

On the day of Judgement, all our deeds will be put on the scales. The good deeds and the bad deeds will be weighed. The greatest good deed is to believe in Allah and to worship Allah alone without making any partners onto Him.

إِيَّاكَ نَعْبُدُ وَإِيَّاكَ نَسْتَعِينُ

(5)   It is You we worship and You we ask for help.

Only Allah has right to be worshipped in truth, Allah has commanded us to worship him. Because Allah is the only Creator, the only Provider, the only one who controls everything in the universe, the one who gives death and life, one who sends the rain from the sky, the one who gives us our health then this is why Allah deserves to be worshipped. We worship Allah by loving Allah more than anything else. If we love Allah we will obey Allah and do what is asked of in the Quran and by the Messenger of Allah ﷺ. We should also fear Allah and not do anything which Allah is not pleased with. We should also have our hope and depend upon Allah when we are unhappy, when we are in a problem and when we are sad. When we need something or we are sad then we ask Allah to help us and give us that which we need from the good things in life.

We don't ask the dead people for help because they cannot hear us nor are they able to do anything for us. The dead people are need of us making Dua for them. We only ask someone for help if they can listen to us and are able to do that which we ask from them. Asking those who cannot hear us, nor help us then this is not allowed this will make Allah angry and by doing this we have made a partner with Allah. Making any partner with Allah will make that person enter the Hellfire.

The House of Allah is called the Masjid which is the place where one performs the prayers. This worship is all for the sake of Allah and we only call upon Allah for help. We do not call others who have

died for help. This picture is the Masjid Al-Nabwi (the Prophet's Masjid) in the city of Madinah, Saudi Arabia. Whoever prays in this masjid will get the reward of 1000 prayers compared to any other masjid. However one prayer in the Grand Masjid of Makkah (Al-Haram) has the reward of 100,000 prayers.

اهْدِنَا الصِّرَاطَ الْمُسْتَقِيمَ

(6) Guide us to the straight path –

This is the best Dua we can make. We are always in need of guidance from Allah, for Allah to show us the true path, for Allah to help us walk on this Straight Path. The Straight Path is the Path with which Allah is happy with. And Allah is happy with His Messenger Muhammad ﷺ and his companions. So this is the path to follow. Follow the way of the first Muslims who helped the Messenger of Allah ﷺ and Allah was pleased with them. So we do not do anything in our religion which is not done by the Companions. The only way to get closer to Allah is to follow the way of the Messenger of Allah ﷺ in the same way as the Companions. All the companions will go to Paradise; they are the best of the people of this Ummah (nation), the ones who best understood the Quran.

In life there are always two paths, one is the correct true Straight path. The other path is the path of lies and falsehood. The Straight Path is that which is according to the Quran and the Sunnah. So this is why knowledge of Islam is important so that the person at every intersection

makes the correct decision. He follows the path of the Messenger of Allah ﷺ and his righteous companions so that he is successful in this life and the Hereafter. The path leading to light is the path of Tawheed, the Quran, and the Sunnah.

صِرَاطَ الَّذِينَ أَنْعَمْتَ عَلَيْهِمْ غَيْرِ الْمَغْضُوبِ عَلَيْهِمْ وَلَا الضَّالِّينَ

(7) The path of those upon whom You have bestowed favor, not of those who have evoked [Your] anger or of those who are astray.

We do not follow those who went on

the wrong path, the path where people followed their desires.

We do not follow anyone except the Messenger of Allah ﷺ. We make sure that all of our actions are according to the the Quran and the Hadith (sayings of the Prophet Muhammed ﷺ). First of all we seek knowledge of something then we act according to this knowledge. The knowledge is which Allah sent down in the form of the Quran and the Sunnah. Whatever is not found in the Quran and the Sunnah or not the way of the Noble Companions then it is not Islamic knowledge, it is something new [a Bidah] which Allah is not pleased with.

It is important to seek knowledge of Islam from the correct sources. Only when a person has knowledge can he act properly according to the Sunnah.

No action is accepted by Allah unless it is done for the sake of Allah (to please Allah) and the action is according to the way of the Prophet ﷺ .

Printed in Great Britain
by Amazon

40920811R00040